To:

_____

From:

_____

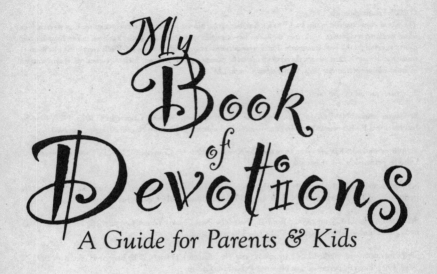

My Book of Devotions

A Guide for Parents & Kids

about Kindness

Simon & Schuster, Inc.

NEW YORK LONDON TORONTO SYDNEY

Simon & Schuster, Inc.

1230 Avenue of the Americas, New York, New York 10020

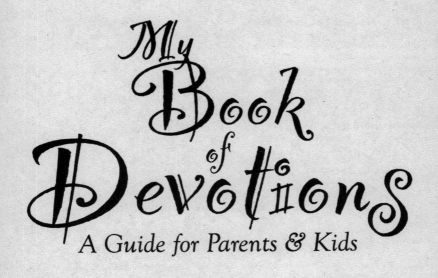

My Book of Devotions

of

A Guide for Parents & Kids

about Kindness

God loves a cheerful giver.

2 Corinthians 9:7 NIV

Table of Contents

A Message for Parents

The fact that you've picked up this book means that you're a concerned, thoughtful parent—congratulations. When you spend time reading to your youngster, you're helping your child build a strong intellectual and spiritual foundation.

This little book—which is intended to be read by Christian parents to their young children—contains 31 brief chapters, one for each day of the month. Each chapter consists of a Bible verse, a brief story or lesson, kid-friendly quotations from notable Christian thinkers, a tip, and a prayer. Every chapter examines a different aspect of an important Biblical theme: kindness.

For the next 31 days, take the time to read one chapter each night to your child, and then spend a few moments talking about the chapter's meaning. By the end of the month, you will have had 31 different opportunities to share God's wisdom with your son or daughter, and that's good.

If you have been touched by God's love and His grace, then you know the joy that He has brought into your own life. Now it's your turn to share His message with the boy or girl whom He has entrusted to your care. Happy reading! And may God richly bless you and your family now and forever.

Kindness Starts with You!

We must not become tired of doing good.
We will receive our harvest of eternal life
at the right time if we do not give up.
Galatians 6:9 NCV

Day 1

Where does kindness start? It starts with you! So if you're waiting for other people to be nice to you before you're nice to them, you've got it backwards. You see, you can never control what other people will say or do, but you can control your own behavior.

The Bible tells us that we should never stop doing good deeds as long as we live. Kindness is God's way, and it should be our way, too. Starting now!

Big Idea for Kids

Kindness every day: Kindness should be part of our lives every day, not just on the days when we feel good. Don't try to be kind some of the time, and don't try to be kind to some of the people you know. Instead, try to be kind all of the time, and try to be kind to all of the people you know.

If we have the true love of God in
our hearts, we will show it in our lives.
We will not have to go up and down
the earth proclaiming it. We will show it
in everything we say or do.
D. L. Moody

Big Idea for Parents

Make Christ the cornerstone: Every family is built upon something; let the foundation of your family be the love of God and the salvation of Christ.

Today's Prayer

Dear Lord, help me to remember
that it is always my job to treat others
with kindness and respect.
Make the Golden Rule my rule,
and make Your Word my guidebook
for the way I treat other people.
Amen

The Golden Rule

Do to others what you want them
to do to you.
Matthew 7:12 NCV

Day 2

Some rules are easier to understand than they are to live by. Jesus told us that we should treat other people in the same way that we would want to be treated: that's the Golden Rule. But sometimes, especially when we're tired or upset, that rule is very hard to follow.

Jesus wants us to treat other people with respect, love, kindness, and courtesy. When we do, we make our families and friends happy . . . and we make our Father in heaven very proud. So if you're wondering how to treat someone else, ask the person you see every time you look into the mirror. The answer you receive will tell you exactly what to do.

Big Idea for Kids

How would you feel? When you're trying to decide how to treat another person, ask yourself this question: "How would I feel if somebody treated me that way?" Then, treat the other person the way that you would want to be treated.

Make the most of today. Translate your good intentions into actual good deeds.

Grenville Kleiser

Big Idea for Parents

Make sure that your Rule is Golden, too: Kids imitate parents, so act accordingly! The best way for your child to learn the Golden Rule is by example . . . your example!

Today's Prayer

Dear Lord, help me always to do
my very best to treat others
as I wish to be treated.
The Golden Rule is Your rule, Father;
let me also make it mine.
Amen

Sharing Your Stuff

God loves the person who gives cheerfully.

2 Corinthians 9:7 NLT

Day 3

How many times have you heard someone say, "Don't touch that; it's mine!"? If you're like most of us, you've heard those words many times, and you may have even said them yourself.

The Bible tells us that it's better for us to share things than it is to keep them all to ourselves. And the Bible also tells us that when we share, it's best to do so cheerfully. So today and every day, let's share. It's the best way because it's God's way.

Big Idea for Kids

Too many toys? Give them away! Are you one of those lucky kids who have more toys than they can play with? If so, remember that not everyone is so lucky. Ask your parents to help you give some of your toys to children who need them more than you do.

All our goodness is a loan; God is the owner.
St. John of the Cross

Big Idea for Parents

Toy referees of the world, unite: It's almost Biblical: when two or more small children are gathered together, they are bound to fuss over toys. Use these disagreements as opportunities to preach the gospel of sharing (even if your sermon falls upon inattentive little ears!).

Today's Prayer

Dear Lord, You have given me so much.
Let me share my gifts with others,
and let me be a joyful and generous
Christian, today and every day.
Amen

Kind Words

When you talk, do not say harmful things.
But say what people need—words that will
help them become stronger. Then what
you say will help those who listen to you.
Ephesians 4:29 ICB

Day 4

Do you like for people to say kind words to you? Of course you do! And that's exactly how other people feel, too. That's why it's so important to say things that make people feel better, not worse.

Your words can help people . . . or not. Make certain that you're the kind of person who says helpful things, not hurtful things. And, make sure that you're the kind of person who helps other people feel better about themselves, not worse.

Everybody needs to hear kind words, and that's exactly the kind of words they should hear from you!

Big Idea for Kids

If you can't think of something nice to say . . . don't say anything. It's better to say nothing than to hurt someone's feelings.

Words. Do you fully understand their power? Can any of us really grasp the mighty force behind the things we say? Do we stop and think before we speak, considering the potency of the words we utter?

Joni Eareckson Tada

Big Idea for Parents

And seldom is heard a discouraging word: If it's good enough for "Home on the Range," it's good enough for your home, too. Make certain that your little abode is a haven of encouragement for every member of your family. You do so by checking your gripes and disappointments at the front door . . . and encouraging everybody else to do likewise!

Today's Prayer

Dear Lord, You hear every word
that I say. Help me remember
to me speak words that are
honest, kind, and helpful.
Amen

Pray About It!

Do not worry about anything.
But pray and ask God for
everything you need.
Philippians 4:6 ICB

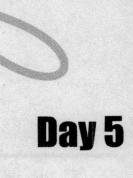

Day 5

If you are upset, pray about it. If you're having trouble being kind to someone, pray about it. If there is a person you don't like, pray for a forgiving heart. If there is something you're worried about, ask God to comfort you. And as you pray more, you'll discover that God is always near and that He's always ready to hear from you. So don't worry about things; pray about them. God is waiting . . . and listening!

Big Idea for Kids

Open-eyed prayers: When you are praying, your eyes don't always have to be closed. Of course, it's good to close your eyes and bow your head, but you can also offer a quick prayer to God with your eyes open. That means that you can pray any time you want.

Prayer is not a weakness but a strength. Its benefits are patience, insight, endurance, and the power to cope with anything.
Franklin Graham

Big Idea for Parents

Make your house a house of prayer: Prayer changes things, and it changes families. Make certain that it changes yours.

Today's Prayer

Dear Lord, You are always near;
let me talk with You often.
Let me use prayer to find
Your answers for my life today
and every day that I live.
Amen

Don't Be Cruel!

Don't ever stop being kind and truthful.
Let kindness and truth show in all you do.
Proverbs 3:3 ICB

Sometimes, young people can be very mean. They can make fun of other people, and when they do so, it's wrong. Period.

As Christians, we should be kind to everyone. And, if other kids say unkind things to a child or make fun of him or her, it's up to us to step in, like the Good Samaritan, and lend a helping hand.

Today and every day, be a person who is known for your kindness, not for your cruelty. That's how God wants you to behave. Period.

Big Idea for Kids

Stand up and be counted! Do you know children who say or do cruel things to other kids? If so, don't join in! Instead, stand up for those who need your help. It's the right thing to do.

> Be so preoccupied with good will that
> you haven't room for ill will.
>
> E. Stanley Jones

Big Idea for Parents

Parents can apologize, too! Nobody's perfect, not even parents! If you say or do something you regret, apologize sooner rather than later. And, if that apology is owed to your spouse or to your child, be humble, be contrite, and be quick about it!

Today's Prayer

Dear Lord, when I see meanness in this
world, let me do my best to correct it.
When I see people who are hurting,
let me do my best to help them.
And when I am hurt by others,
let me do my best to forgive them.

Amen

His Name Was Barnabas

Barnabas was a good man,
full of the Holy Spirit and full of faith.
Acts 11:23-24 ICB

Day 7

Barnabas was a leader in the early Christian church who was known for his kindness and for his ability to encourage others. Because of Barnabas, many people were introduced to Christ.

We become like Barnabas when we speak kind words to our families and to our friends. And then, because we have been generous and kind, the people around us can see how Christians should behave. So when in doubt, be kind and generous to others, just like Barnabas.

Big Idea for Kids

Be an encourager! Barnabas was known as a man who encouraged others. In other words, he made other people feel better by saying kind things. You, like Barnabas, can encourage your family and friends . . . and you should.

Make it a rule, and pray to God to help you to keep it, never to lie down at night without being able to say: "I have made at least one human being a little wiser, a little happier, or a little better this day."

Charles Kingsley

Big Idea for Parents

Parents make the best encouragers! You're not just your children's parents; you're their biggest fans. Make sure they know it.

Today's Prayer

Dear Lord, let me help to encourage
other people by the words that I say
and the things that I do. Let me be
a person who is always helpful and kind
to my friends and family. And let them
see Your love for me reflected
in my love for them.
Amen

Pray for People Who Aren't Nice

I tell you, love your enemies.
Pray for those who hurt you.
If you do this, you will be true sons
of your Father in heaven.
Matthew 6:44-45 ICB

Day 8

It's easy to love people who have been nice to you, but it's very hard to love people who have treated you badly. Still, Jesus instructs us to treat both our friends and our enemies with kindness and respect.

Are you having problems being nice to someone? Is there someone you know whom you don't like very much? Remember that Jesus not only forgave His enemies, He also loved them . . . and so should you.

Big Idea for Kids

Making up may not be as hard as you think! If there is someone who has been mean to you, perhaps it's time for the two of you to make up. If you're willing to be the first person to offer a kind word, you'll discover that making up is usually easier than you think.

You can be sure you are abiding in Christ if you are able to have a Christlike love toward the people that irritate you the most.

Vonette Bright

Big Idea for Parents

Forgive . . . and keep forgiving! Sometimes, you may forgive someone once and then, at a later time, become angry at the very same person again. If so, you must forgive that person again and again . . . until it sticks!

Today's Prayer

Dear Lord, give me a forgiving heart.
When I have bad feelings toward
another person, help me to forgive
them and to love them, just as
You forgive and love me.
Amen

Do Yourself a Favor

A kind person is doing himself a favor.
But a cruel person brings
trouble upon himself.
Proverbs 11:17 ICB

King Solomon wrote most of the Book of Proverbs; in it, he gave us wonderful advice for living wisely. Solomon warned that unkind behavior leads only to trouble, but kindness is its own reward.

The next time you're tempted to say an unkind word, remember Solomon. He was one of the wisest men who ever lived, and he knew that it's always better to be kind. And now, you know it, too.

Big Idea for Kids

Sorry you said it? Apologize! Did you say something that hurt someone's feelings? Then it's time for an apology: yours. It's never too late to apologize, but it's never too early either!

Always be a little kinder than necessary.

James Barrie

Big Idea for Parents

Mirror, mirror, on the wall: When you look into the mirror, you're gazing at the person who is the primary role model for your child. It's a big responsibility, but you—and God—are up to it!

Today's Prayer

Dear Lord, let me be a kind person.
Let me be quick to share and quick to
forgive. And when I make mistakes,
let me be quick to change and
quick to ask forgiveness from
others and from You.
Amen

The Good Samaritan

Carry each other's burdens,
and in this way you will fulfill
the law of Christ.
Galatians 6:2 NIV

Jesus told the story of a Jewish man who had been attacked by robbers. Luckily, a kind Samaritan happened by. And even though Jews and Samaritans were enemies, the Samaritan rescued the injured man.

And the meaning of the story is this: Jesus wants us to be kind to everyone, not just to our families and our friends. Jesus wants us to be good neighbors to all people, not just to those who are exactly like us.

Are you a good Samaritan? If so, you're doing the right thing, and that's exactly how God wants you to behave.

Big Idea for Kids

Look around: Someone very near you may need a helping hand or a kind word, so keep your eyes open, and look for people who need your help, whether at home, at church, or at school.

No one stands taller in the climb
to success than when he bends over
to help up someone else.
John Maxwell

Big Idea for Parents

Preach, teach, and reach . . . out!: When it comes to teaching our children about helping others, our sermons are not as important as our service. Charity should start at home—with parents—and work its way down the family tree from there.

Today's Prayer

Dear Lord, make me a Good Samaritan.
Let me never be too busy or too proud
to help a person in need. You have
given me so many blessings, Lord.
Let me share those blessings
with others today and
every day that I live.
Amen

When People Aren't Nice

If someone does wrong to you,
do not pay him back by doing wrong to him.
Try to do what everyone thinks is right.
Romans 12:17 NCV

Sometimes people aren't nice, and that's when we feel like striking back in anger. But the Bible tells us not to do it. As Christians, we should not repay one bad deed with another bad deed. Instead, we should forgive the other person as quickly as we can.

Are you angry at someone? If so, then it's time to forgive him or her. Jesus does not intend that your heart be troubled by anger. Your heart should instead be filled with love, just as Jesus' heart was . . . and is!

Big Idea for Kids

Forgive . . . and keep forgiving! Sometimes, you may forgive someone once and then, at a later time, become angry at the very same person again. If so, you must forgive that person again and again . . . until it sticks!

> Keep away from people who try
> to belittle your ambitions.
> Mark Twain

Big Idea for Parents

Holding a grudge? Drop it! How can you expect your kids to forgive others if you don't? Never expect your children to be more forgiving than you are.

Today's Prayer

Dear Lord, whenever I am angry,
give me a forgiving heart.
And help me remember that
the best day to forgive
somebody is this one.
Amen

Paul and His Friends

I thank my God every time I remember you.
Philippians 1:3 NIV

Day 12

In his letter to the Philippians, Paul wrote to his distant friends saying that he thanked God every time He remembered them. We, too, should thank God for the family and friends He has brought into our lives.

Today, let's give thanks to God for all the people who love us, for brothers and sisters, parents and grandparents, aunts and uncles, cousins, and friends. And then, as a way of thanking God, let's obey Him by being especially kind to our loved ones. They deserve it, and so does He.

Big Idea for Kids

The mailman can help: If you have friends or relatives who are far away, send them letters or drawings (your mom or dad will be happy to mail them for you). Everybody loves to receive mail, and so will your family members and friends.

When friends meet, hearts warm.

Anonymous

Big Idea for Parents

Help start the letter-writing habit early: Encourage your children to become world-class letter writers and top-flight "thank- you" note senders. Even in this age of electronic communication, nothing can take the place of an old-fashioned letter. And besides, without our children's notes and artwork, how would we decorate our refrigerators?

Today's Prayer

Dear Lord, thank you for my family and
my friends. Let me show kindness to
all of them: those who are here
at home and those who are far away.
Then, my family and friends will know
that I remember them and love them,
today and every day.

Amen

Be Honest and Kind

Good people will be guided by honesty.

Proverbs 11:3 ICB

Day 13

Maybe you've heard this phrase: "Honesty is the best policy." But, honesty is not just the best policy; it is also God's policy.

An important part of becoming a good person is learning to tell the truth. Lies usually have a way of hurting people, so even when it's hard, we must be honest with others.

If we are going to follow the rules that God has given us, we must remember that truth is not just the best way; it is also His way. So be honest and kind . . . now!

Big Idea for Kids

Honesty in Action: Thinking about being an honest person isn't enough. If you want to be considered an honest person, you must tell the truth today and every day.

> Honesty is the first chapter
> in the book of wisdom.
> Thomas Jefferson

Big Idea for Parents

Coaching kids on what to say (and what not to say): We live in a world where common courtesy is all too uncommon. That's why it's important to teach our children about the importance of courtesy and tact. Does this sound old-fashioned? It's not! It's simply responsible parenting.

Today's Prayer

Dear Lord, sometimes it's hard to tell the truth. But even when telling the truth is difficult, let me follow Your commandment. Honesty isn't just the best policy, Lord; it's Your policy, and I will obey You by making it my policy, too.

Amen

Let's Make Friends!

A friend loves you all the time.
Proverbs 17:17 ICB

Day 14

The Bible tells us that friendship can be a wonderful thing. That's why it's good to know how to make and to keep good friends.

If you want to make lots of friends, practice the Golden Rule with everybody you know. Be kind. Share. Say nice things. Be helpful. When you do, you'll discover that the Golden Rule isn't just a nice way to behave; it's also a great way to make and to keep friends!

Big Idea for Kids

First, become interested in them . . .and soon they'll become interested in you!

The best times in life are made
a thousand times better when shared
with a dear friend.
Luci Swindoll

Big Idea for Parents

Help from the sidelines: As parents, we can't make friendships for our children, but we can coach them on the art of making friends. All of us, whether youngsters or grown-ups, make friends by treating others as we wish to be treated. And if that sounds suspiciously like the Golden Rule, that's because it is the Golden Rule.

Today's Prayer

Dear Lord, help me to be a good friend.
Let me treat other people as I want
to be treated. Let me share my things,
and let me share kind words
with my friends and family,
today and every day.
Amen

Making Other People Feel Better!

Let us think about each other and help each other to show love and do good deeds.
Hebrews 10:24 ICB

Day 15

When other people are sad, what can we do? We can do our best to cheer them up by showing kindness and love.

The Bible tells us that we must care for each other, and when everybody is happy, that's an easy thing to do. But, when people are sad, for whatever reason, it's up to us to speak a kind word or to offer a helping hand.

Do you know someone who is discouraged or sad? If so, perhaps it's time to take matters into your own hands. Think of something you can do to cheer that person up . . . and then do it! You'll make two people happy.

Big Idea for Kids

Cheering someone up without saying a word: If you want to cheer someone up but can't think of something to say or do, try drawing a picture or writing a note.

> What this old world needs is less advice
> and more helping hands.
>
> Anonymous

Big Idea for Parents

Parents set the verbal tone: As parents, it's up to us to establish the general tone of the conversations that occur in our homes. Let's make certain that the tone we set is worthy of the One we worship.

Today's Prayer

Dear Lord, make me a loving,
encouraging Christian. And, let my love
for Jesus be reflected through
the kindness that I show to those
who need the healing touch
of the Master's hand.
Amen

Be Kind to Parents

Honor your father and your mother.
Exodus 20:12 ICB

Day 16

We love our parents so very much, but sometimes, we may take them for granted. When we take them "for granted," that means that we don't give them the honor and respect they deserve.

The Bible tells us to honor our parents. That's God's rule, and it's also the best way to live. When we treat our parents with the respect they deserve, we show them that we appreciate all they have done for us. And that's so much better than taking our parents for granted, and if you don't believe it, just ask them!

Big Idea for Kids

Two magic words: Thank you!: Your parents will never become tired of hearing those two little words. And while you're at it, try three more: "I love you!"

Showing kindness to others is one of the nicest things we can do for ourselves.

Janette Oke

Big Idea for Parents

Old-fashioned respect never goes out of fashion: Remember the good old days when children were polite and respectful, especially to adults? For wise parents, those good old days are now.

Today's Prayer

Dear Lord, make me respectful
and thankful. Let me give honor
and love to my parents,
and let my behavior be pleasing
to them . . . and to You.
Amen

It's Time to Be Cheerful

A happy heart is like a continual feast.
Proverbs 15:15 NCV

Day 17

What is a continual feast? It's a little bit like a non-stop birthday party: fun, fun, and more fun! The Bible tells us that a cheerful heart can make life like a continual feast, and that's something worth working for.

Where does cheerfulness begin? It begins inside each of us; it begins in the heart. So today and every day, let's be thankful to God for His blessings, and let's show our thanks by sharing good cheer wherever we go. This old world needs all the cheering up it can get . . . and so do we!

Big Idea for Kids

Cheer up somebody else. Do you need a little cheering up? If so, find somebody else who needs cheering up, too. Then, do your best to brighten that person's day. When you do, you'll discover that cheering up other people is a wonderful way to cheer yourself up too.

Cheerfulness strengthens the heart and makes us try harder to have a good life, thus God's servants must always be in good spirits.

St. Philip Neri

Big Idea for Parents

Make time for "family cheering up" caravans: Do you know someone who is homebound or hospitalized? Take the kids along for a brief visit. Your children will learn that the Golden Rule requires us to reach out to those who need our encouragement and our love.

Today's Prayer

Dear Lord, make me a cheerful
Christian. Today, let me celebrate
my blessings and my life; let me be
quick to smile and slow to become
angry. And, let Your love shine
in me and through me.
Amen

Be Kind to Everyone

Exercise your freedom by serving God, not by breaking rules. Treat everyone you meet with dignity. Love your spiritual family. Revere God. Respect the government.

1 Peter 2:16-17 MSG

Who deserves our respect? Grown-ups? Of course. Teachers? Certainly. Family members? Yes. Friends? That's right, but it doesn't stop there. The Bible teaches us to treat all people with respect.

Respect for others is habit-forming: the more we do it, the easier it becomes. So start practicing right now. Say lots of kind words and do lots of kind things, because when it comes to kindness and respect, practice makes perfect.

Big Idea for Kids

Respecting all kinds of people: Make sure that you show proper respect for everyone, even if that person happens to be different from you. It's easy to make fun of people who seem different . . . but it's wrong.

What is your focus today?
Joy comes when it is Jesus first,
others second . . . then you.
Kay Arthur

Big Idea for Parents

It starts with you: Remember: Kindness, dignity, and respect for others begin at the head of the household and work their way down from there. And our kids are always watching!

Today's Prayer

Dear Lord, help me to be kind
to everyone I meet. Help me to be
respectful to all people, not just
teachers and parents. Help me to say
kind words and do good deeds,
today and every day.
Amen

Say a Kind Word

The right word spoken at the right time is as beautiful as gold apples in a silver bowl.
Proverbs 25:11 ICB

Day 19

How hard is it to speak with kind words? Not very! Yet sometimes we're so busy that we forget to say the very things that might make other people feel better.

We should always try to say nice things to our families and friends. And when we feel like saying something that's not so nice, perhaps we should stop and think before we say it. Kind words help; cruel words hurt. It's as simple as that. And, when we say the right thing at the right time, we give a gift that can change someone's day or someone's life.

Big Idea for Kids

If you don't know what to say . . . don't say anything. Sometimes, a hug works better than a whole mouthful of words.

Kind words can be short and easy to speak, but their echoes are truly endless.

Mother Teresa

Big Idea for Parents

Kindness is contagious: kids can catch it from their parents.

Today's Prayer

Dear Lord, help me to say
the right thing at the right time.
Let me choose my words carefully
so that I can help other people
and glorify You.
Amen

God Knows the Heart

I am the Lord, and I can look
into a person's heart.
Jeremiah 17:10 ICB

Day 20

You can try to keep secrets from other people, but you can't keep secrets from God. God knows what you think and what you do. And, if you want to please God, you must start with good intentions and a kind heart.

If your heart tells you not to do something, don't do it! If your conscience tells you that something is wrong, stop! If you feel ashamed by something you've done, don't do it ever again! You can keep secrets from other people some of the time, but God is watching all of the time, and He sees everything, including your heart.

Big Idea for Kids

That little voice inside your head . . . is called your conscience. Listen to it; it's usually right!

Our actions are seen by people,
but our motives are monitored by God.
Franklin Graham

Big Idea for Parents

Teaching values: Your children will learn about life from many sources; the most important source can and should be you. But remember that the lectures you give are never as important as the ones you live.

Today's Prayer

Dear Lord, other people see me from
the outside, but You know my heart.
Let my heart be pure, and let me listen
to the voice that You have placed
there, today and always.
Amen

Let's Be Gentle

Pleasant words are like a honeycomb.
They make a person happy and healthy.
Proverbs 16:24 ICB

Day 21

The Bible says that using gentle words is helpful and that using cruel words is not. But sometimes, especially when we're frustrated or angry, our words and our actions may not be so gentle. Sometimes, we may say things or do things that are unkind or hurtful to others. When we do, we're wrong.

So the next time you're tempted to strike out in anger, don't. And if you want to help your family and friends, remember that gentle words are better than harsh words and good deeds are better than the other kind. Always!

Big Idea for Kids

Count to ten . . . and keep counting: If you're mad at someone, don't say the first thing that comes to your mind and don't strike out in anger. Instead, catch your breath and start counting until you are once again in control of your temper. If you get to a million and you're still counting, go to bed! You'll feel better in the morning.

Nothing is so strong as gentleness;
nothing is so gentle as real strength.
St. Francis de Sales

Big Idea for Parents

Rest, rest, rest . . . Oftentimes, our anger is nothing more than exhaustion in disguise. When in doubt, get eight hours of sleep.

Today's Prayer

Dear Lord, help me to keep away from
angry thoughts and angry people.
And if I am tempted to have a temper
tantrum, help to calm down before I do.
Amen

Telling Tales

A person who gossips ruins friendships.
Proverbs 16:28 ICB

Day 22

Do you know what gossip is? It's when we say bad things about people who are not around. When we gossip, we hurt others and we hurt ourselves. That's why the Bible tells us that gossip is wrong.

Sometimes, it's tempting to say bad things about people, and when we do, it makes us feel important . . . for a while. But, after a while, the bad things that we say come back to hurt us, and, of course, they hurt other people, too.

So if you want to be a kind person and a good friend, don't gossip . . . and don't listen to people who do.

Big Idea for Kids

Watch what you say: Don't say something behind someone's back that you wouldn't say to that person directly.

We have in Jesus Christ a perfect example of how to put God's truth into practice.

Bill Bright

Big Idea for Parents

Make your home a gossip-free zone: Gossip is a learned behavior. Make sure that your kids don't learn it from you!

Today's Prayer

Dear Lord, I know that I have
influence on many people . . .
make me an influence for good.
And let the words that I speak
today be worthy of the One
who has saved me forever.
Amen

The Things We Say

A good person's words will help many others.
Proverbs 10:21 ICB

Day 23

The words that we speak are very important because of how they affect other people. The things that we say can either help people or hurt them. We can either make people feel better, or we can hurt their feelings.

The Bible reminds us that words are powerful things; we must use them carefully. Let's use our words to help our families and friends. When we do, we make their lives better and our own.

Big Idea for Kids

Think first, speak second: If you want to keep from hurting other people's feelings, don't open your mouth until you've turned on your brain.

> The battle of the tongue is won not
> in the mouth, but in the heart.
> Annie Chapman

Big Idea for Parents

When kids are mean: Face it: even the most angelic children can do things that are unfair or unkind. When we observe such behavior in our own children, we must be understanding, but firm. We live in a world where misbehavior is tolerated and, in many cases, glorified. But inside the walls of our own homes, misbehavior should never be ignored; it should be corrected by loving, courageous parents.

Today's Prayer

Dear Lord, make my words pleasing to You. Let the words that I say and the things that I do help others to feel better about themselves and to know more about You.

Amen

When You're Angry

A foolish person loses his temper.
But a wise person controls his anger.

Proverbs 29:11 ICB

Day 24

Temper tantrums are so silly. And so is pouting. So, of course, is whining. When we lose our tempers, we say things that we shouldn't say, and we do things that we shouldn't do. Too bad!

The Bible tells us that it is foolish to become angry and that it is wise to remain calm. That's why we should learn to control our tempers before our tempers control us.

Big Idea for Kids

No more temper tantrums! If you think you're about to throw a tantrum, slow down, catch your breath, and walk away if you must. It's better to walk away than it is to strike out in anger.

Why lose your temper if, by doing so,
you offend God, annoy other people,
give yourself a bad time . . . and, in the end,
have to find it again?

Josemaria Escriva

Big Idea for Parents

Parents get angry, too: as bad as children's temper tantrums can be, they pale in comparison to the adult versions. If you expect your children to control their tempers—and you should—then you, as the adult in the family, must also control yours.

Today's Prayer

Dear Lord, I can be so impatient, and I can become so angry. Calm me down, Lord, and make me a patient, forgiving Christian. Just as You have forgiven me, let me forgive others so that I can follow the example of Your Son.

Amen

When Other People Need Help

I tell you the truth, anything you did
for even the least of my people here,
you also did for me.
Matthew 25:40 NCV

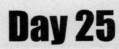
Day 25

Perhaps you have lots of advantages. Some people don't. Perhaps you have the benefit of a loving family, a strong faith in God, and three good meals each day. Some people don't. Perhaps you were lucky enough to be born into a country where people are free. Some people weren't.

Jesus instructed us to care for those who can't care for themselves, wherever they may be. And, when we do something nice for someone in need, we have also done a good deed for our Savior. So today, look for someone who needs your help, and then do your best to help him or her. God is watching and waiting. The next move is yours.

Big Idea for Kids

When am I old enough to start giving? If you're old enough to understand these words, you're old enough to start giving to your church and to those who are less fortunate than you. If you're not sure about the best way to do it, ask your parents!

Encouraging others means helping people, looking for the best in them, and trying to bring out their positive qualities.

John Maxwell

Big Idea for Parents

Teaching generosity: It's never too early to emphasize the importance of giving. From the time that a child is old enough to drop a penny into the offering plate, we, as parents, should stress the obligation that we all have to share the blessings that God has shared with us.

Today's Prayer

Dear Lord, You have given me so
many blessings. Make me a cheerful,
generous giver, Lord, as I share
the blessings that You first
shared with me.
Amen

How To Be Happy

Blessed are those who hunger and thirst for
righteousness, because they will be filled.

Matthew 5:6 HCSB

Day 26

Do you want to be happy? Here are some things you should do: Love God and His Son, Jesus; obey the Golden Rule; and always try to do the right thing. When you do these things, you'll discover that happiness goes hand in hand with good behavior.

The happiest people do not misbehave; the happiest people are not cruel or greedy. The happiest people don't say unkind things. The happiest people are those who love God and follow his rules—starting, of course, with the Golden one.

Big Idea for Kids

Sometimes happy, sometimes not: Even if you're a very good person, you shouldn't expect to be happy all the time. Sometimes, things will happen to make you sad, and it's okay to be sad when bad things happen to you or to your friends and family. But remember: through good times and bad, you'll always be happier if you obey the rules of your Father in heaven. So obey them!

> People are just about as happy
> as they make up their minds to be.
> Abraham Lincoln

Big Idea for Parents

Happiness at home: Your children deserve to grow up in a happy home . . . and you owe it to them (and to yourself) to provide that kind of home.

Today's Prayer

Dear Lord, make me the kind of
Christian who earns happiness by
doing the right thing. When I obey
your rules, Father, I will find the joy
that you have in store for me. Let me
find Your joy, Lord, today and always.
Amen

What James Said

This royal law is found in the Scriptures:
"Love your neighbor as yourself."
If you obey this law,
then you are doing right.
James 2:8 ICB

Day 27

James was the brother of Jesus and a leader of the early Christian church. In a letter that is now a part of the New Testament, James reminded his friends of a "royal law." That law is the Golden Rule.

When we treat others in the same way that we wish to be treated, we are doing the right thing. James knew it and so, of course, did his brother Jesus. Now we should learn the same lesson: it's nice to be nice; it's good to be good; and it's great to be kind.

Big Idea for Kids

Kind is as kind does: In order to be a kind person, you must do kind things. Thinking about them isn't enough. So get busy! Your family and friends need all the kindness they can get!

> Be enthusiastic. Every occasion is
> an opportunity to do good.
> Russell Conwell

Big Idea for Parents

It's up to us: Our children will learn about Jesus at church and, in some cases, at school. But, the ultimate responsibility for religious teachings should never be delegated to institutions outside the home. As parents, we must teach our children about the love and grace of Jesus Christ by our words and by our actions.

Today's Prayer

Dear Lord, it's easy to be kind to some people and difficult to be kind to others. Let me be kind to all people so that I might follow in the footsteps of Your Son.
Amen

Doing What's Right

Doing what is right brings freedom
to honest people.
Proverbs 11:6 ICB

Day 28

Sometimes, it's so much easier to do the wrong thing than it is to do the right thing, especially when we're tired or frustrated. But, doing the wrong thing almost always leads to trouble. And sometimes, it leads to BIG trouble.

When you do the right thing, you don't have to worry about what you did or what you said. But, when you do the wrong thing, you'll be worried that someone will find out. So do the right thing, which, by the way, also happens to be the kind thing. You'll be glad you did, and so will other people!

Big Idea for Kids

Think ahead: Before you do something, ask yourself this question: "Will I be ashamed if my parents find out?" If the answer to that question is "Yes," don't do it!

The time is always right to do what is right.
Martin Luther King, Jr.

Big Idea for Parents

See as much as you can; correct as much as you should: Encouraging children to do the right thing requires an observing eye and a patient heart. Expect your children to be well-behaved, but don't expect them to be perfect. In fact, an important part of parenting is knowing what to overlook and when to overlook it.

Today's Prayer

Dear Lord, I want to be a person who
respects others, and I want to be
a person who is kind. Wherever I am
and whatever I do, let me be like Jesus
in the way that I treat others, because
with Him as my guide, I will do
the right thing, today and forever.

Amen

It Starts in the Heart

Those who are pure in their thinking are happy, because they will be with God.

Matthew 5:8 NCV

Day 29

Where does kindness start? It starts in our hearts and works its way out from there. Jesus taught us that a pure heart is a wonderful blessing. It's up to each of us to fill our hearts with love for God, love for Jesus, and love for all people. When we do, we are blessed.

Do you want to be the best person you can be? Then invite the love of Christ into your heart and share His love with your family and friends. And remember that lasting love always comes from a pure heart . . . like yours!

Big Idea for Kids

Learn about Jesus and His attitude. Then try and do what Jesus would do.

> The God who dwells in heaven is
> willing to dwell also in the heart
> of the humble believer.
>
> Warren Wiersbe

Big Idea for Parents

Jesus loves you, this you know . . . and they should, too! Of course you know that Jesus loves you. But it's up to you to make sure that they know that you know. So remind them often.

Today's Prayer

Dear Lord, give me a heart that is pure.
Let me live by Your Word and trust in
Your Son today and forever.
Amen

Growing Up with God

He will teach us of his ways,
and we will walk in his paths.
Isaiah 2:3 KJV

Day 30

When will you stop growing up? Hopefully never! If you keep studying God's Word and obeying His commandments, you will never be a "fully grown" Christian. You will always be a "growing" Christian.

God knows you can't be perfect, but He doesn't want you to keep doing bad things either! Instead, God wants you to keep growing in the love and knowledge of His Son. When you do, you'll keep on growing, and that's exactly the kind of Christian that God wants you to become.

Big Idea for Kids

Daily Devotionals? Yes! Try your best to read the Bible with your parents every day. If they forget, remind them!

> With God, it isn't who you were
> that matters; it's who you are becoming.
> Liz Curtis Higgs

Big Idea for Parents

Making time for God: Our days are filled to the brim with obligations and priorities, but no priority is greater than our obligation to our Creator. Let's make sure that we give Him the time He deserves, not only on Sundays, but also on every other day of the week.

Today's Prayer

Dear Lord, let me always keep learning about Your love and about Your Son, Jesus. Make me a better person today than I was yesterday, and let me continue to grow as a Christian every day that I live.

Amen

God Is Love

My beloved friends, let us continue to love each other since love comes from God. Everyone who loves is born of God and experiences a relationship with God. The person who refuses to love doesn't know the first thing about God, because God is love—so you can't know him if you don't love.

1 John 4:8 MSG

The Bible tells us that God is love and that if we wish to know Him, we must have love in our hearts. Sometimes, of course, when we're tired, frustrated, or angry, it is very hard for us to be loving. Thankfully, anger and frustration are feelings that come and go, but God's love lasts forever.

If you'd like to improve your day and your life, share God's love with your family and friends. Every time you love, every time you are kind, and every time you give, God smiles.

Big Idea for Kids

Show and Tell: It's good to tell your loved ones how you feel about them, but that's not enough. You should also show them how you feel with your good deeds and your kind words.

If God had a refrigerator, your picture would be on it. If he had a wallet, your photo would be in it. He sends you flowers every spring and a sunrise every morning.

Max Lucado

Big Idea for Parents

Be expressive: Make certain that at your house, love is expressed and demonstrated many times each day. Little acts of consideration and kindness can make a big difference in the way that your child views the world.

Today's Prayer

Dear Lord, make me a person who is loving and giving. You first loved me, Father. Let me, in turn, love others, and let my behavior show them that I love them, today and forever.

Amen

Bible Verses to Remember

Love is patient; love is kind.

1 Corinthians 13:4 HCSB

Honor your father and your mother.

Exodus 20:12 ICB

For God so loved the world that
he gave his one and only Son,
that whoever believes in him shall not
perish but have eternal life.

John 3:16 NIV

Do not worry about anything. But pray and ask God for everything you need.

Philippians 4:6 ICB

So always do these things:
Show mercy to others,
be kind, humble, gentle,
and patient.

Colossians 3:12 NCV

If someone does
wrong to you,
do not pay him back
by doing wrong to him.

Romans 12:17 ICB

Love other people just as Christ loved us.

Ephesians 5:2 ICB

Now these three remain: faith, hope, and love. But the greatest of these is love.

1 Corinthians 13:13 HCSB

Do for other people
the same things you want
them to do for you.

Matthew 7:12 ICB

We must not become tired of
doing good. We will receive our harvest
of eternal life at the right time.
We must not give up!

Galatians 6:9 ICB

We must obey God rather than men.

Acts 5:29 NASB

Make the most of every opportunity.

Colossians 4:5 NIV

A new commandment I give to you,
that you love one another;
as I have loved you,
that you also love one another.

John 13:34 NKJV

God loves the person who gives cheerfully.

2 Corinthians 9:7 NLT

A cheerful heart is good medicine.

Proverbs 17:22 NIV

Your heart must not be troubled. Believe in God; believe also in Me.

John 14:1 HCSB

If you have two shirts,
share with the person
who does not have one.
If you have food,
share that too.

Luke 3:11 ICB